First World War
and Army of Occupation
War Diary
France, Belgium and Germany

2 DIVISION
6 Infantry Brigade
Herefordshire Regiment
1/1st Battalion
2 August 1915 - 29 February 1916

WO95/1358/2

The Naval & Military Press Ltd
www.nmarchive.com
Published in association with The National Archives

Published by

The Naval & Military Press Ltd

Unit 10 Ridgewood Industrial Park,

Uckfield, East Sussex,

TN22 5QE England

Tel: +44 (0) 1825 749494

www.naval-military-press.com

www.nmarchive.com

This diary has been reprinted in facsimile from the original. Any imperfections are inevitably reproduced and the quality may fall short of modern type and cartographic standards.

© **Crown Copyright**
Images reproduced by permission of The National Archives, London, England, 2015.

Contents

Document type	Place/Title	Date From	Date To
Heading	WO95/1358/2		
Heading	2nd Division 6th Infy Bde 1st Battalion Hertfordshire Regt. 1915 Aug-Feb 1916 From 4 Bde 2, Div 39,Div 118 Bde		
Heading	2nd Division War Diaries 1st Battn. Herts Regt. From August, To December 1915		
Heading	6th Infantry Brigade 2nd Division War Diary 1st Battn. The Hertfordshire Regiment August 1915		
War Diary		02/08/1915	31/08/1915
Heading	6th Infantry Brigade 2nd Division War Diary 1st Battn. The Hertfordshire Regiment. September 1915		
War Diary		04/09/1915	30/09/1915
Heading	6th Infantry Brigade 2nd Division War Diary 1st Battn. The Hertfordshire Regiment October 1915		
War Diary		01/10/1915	31/10/1915
Heading	6th Infantry Brigade 2nd Division War Diary 1st Battn. The Hertfordshire Regiment. November 1915		
War Diary		01/11/1915	29/11/1915
Heading	6th Infantry Brigade 2nd Division War Diary 1st Battn. The Hertfordshire Regiment. December 1915		
War Diary		02/12/1915	27/12/1915
Heading	6th Brigade 2nd Division 1st Battalion Hertfordshire Regiment January 1916		
War Diary		27/12/1915	30/01/1916
War Diary		03/01/1916	07/01/1916
Heading	6th Brigade 2nd Division Battalion Went To G. H.Q. 21st February 19161st Battalion Hertfordshire Regiment February 1916		
War Diary		02/02/1916	29/02/1916

WO 95/1358/2

2ND DIVISION
6TH INFY BDE

1ST BATTALION

HERTFORDSHIRE REGT.

1915 AUG ~~JAN~~ - FEB 1916.

FROM 4 BDE 2, DIV

To 39 DIV 116 BDE

2nd Division 6 BDE

War Diaries

1st Battn. Herts Regt.

From August, To December 1915

6th Infantry Brigade.
2nd Division.

(Battn. joined Bde. from
4th Guards Bde. when latter
left Div. on 19.8.15)

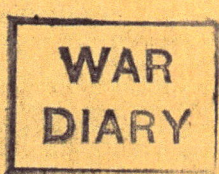

1st BATTN. THE HERTFORDSHIRE REGIMENT.

A U G U S T

1 9 1 5

1st Bn Hertfordshire Regt T.F. **22**

War Diary for Aug. 1915

August. 2. The Battalion was relieved by the 2nd Coldstream Guards and marched back into billets at LE QUESNOY.

" 4 Thirty five N.C.O's and men joined the Battalion.
The Battalion relieved the 2nd Coldstream Guards in B.3.

" 6. We were relieved by the 3rd Coldstream Guards.

" 8. Battalion relieved the 2nd Coldstream Guards.

" 10 Relieved by the 3rd Coldstream Guards.

" 12. Relieved the 2nd Coldstream Guards.

" 15. The Battalion was relieved by the 2nd Battalion Worcestershire Regt on the 1st (Guards) Brigade being relieved by 5th Brigade. Battalion marched back into billets at BEUVRY.

" 19. Battalion left the 1st (Guards) Brigade. One Company marched into BETHUNE to bid farewell to the Guards.

" 15 In Billets at BEUVRY

Aug. 24. Battalion marched back into Billets at VENDIN.

" 27. Battalion went into bivouacs at GORRE to dig new communication trench from PONT FIXE – WINDY CORNER road to junction of WHITEHALL and HATFIELD ROAD. Headquarters etc remaining at VENDIN.
Casualties – one man killed, two wounded while digging.
Amongst the Russian Awards appearing in the Press it was stated that No. 2080 Pte R. Redding, and 1342 Pte J.W. Wilkinson had been awarded the Medal of St George. 3rd Class.

" 30. Headquarters etc marched from VENDIN into MONTMORENCY BARRACKS BETHUNE

" 31. HQrs in billets at BETHUNE, BATTALION still engaged digging new Trench.

31 8 15

Adg. Adjt 1st Bn Herts Regt.

6th Infantry Brigade.
2nd Division.

1st BATTN. THE HERTFORDSHIRE REGIMENT.

S E P T E M B E R

1 9 1 5

1st Bn Herts Regt (T.F.)

War Diary for September 1915

Sept 1. Battalion marched to CAMBRIN, one Company in CUINCHY SUPPORT POINT, one Company in CAMBRIN SUPPORT POINT one Company MAISON ROUGE dugouts and one Company in ANNEQUIN.

6. Headquarters moved from CAMBRIN to ANNEQUIN

8. The Battalion moved into Z 2 Section and relieved the 1st Bn Kings Royal Rifles.
Casualties during four days were –
2nd Lieut N P GOLD wounded, one man killed and 3 wounded

12. Battalion was relieved by 1st Bn Kings Royal Rifles and marched back into billets at BEUVRY

16. The Battalion relieved 1st Kings in A.1. Section.

19. The Battalion was relieved by the 1st Kings in A.1 Section

20. Battalion relieved 1st Kings in A.1. Section.

22. 2nd Lieut Ince and 2nd Lieut Smallwood joined the Battalion from the 3rd Battalion

1915
Oct 24th The Battalion was relieved by the 1st Kings in A.1. Sectors, two Companies No 2 and No 3 at BRADDELL POINT, No 1 Co. CAMBRIN SUPPORT POINT, No 4 Co. STAFFORD REDOUBT.

25. At 6.30 a.m. the 1st Kings attacked but never reached the Germans Trenches as they were held up by heavy machine gun fire and No 3 and No 4 Companies who were in close support were ordered not to advance. We then assumed normal conditions.

26. We relieved half of the Kings line with one Company.

27. At 5 p.m. we made another gas attack, on the enemy as on the 25th but were ordered not to advance unless the enemy had suffered from it.
At 5.30 p.m. we sent out a patrol but they were immediately fired at by enemy machine guns and in consequence we did not attack, neither did the 1st Kings.
From 25th to 30th our casualties were approximately Captain

1915
Smeathman wounded, Capt Times
wounded, Lieut Molony suffering from
gas poisoning, other ranks wounded
or suffering from gas. 25.

Sept 30. The 6th Brigade was relieved

Sept 30. The 6th Brigade was relieved the
Battalion being relieved by the 9th
Bn CHESHIRE REGT. and marched
back into billets in the eastern end of
BETHUNE.

Berem Lieut & Adjt
1st Bn Herts Regt

6th Infantry Brigade.
2nd Division.

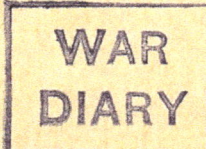

1st BATTN. THE HERTFORDSHIRE REGIMENT.

OCTOBER

1915

1st B. Hertfordshire Regt. T.
War Diary for October 1915

Oct. 1. Battalion went into the Trenches in the front of VERMELLES, north of the HULLOCK ROAD, being in support of the 1st Bn KINGS ROYAL RIFLES who were holding the old front line GERMAN Trench which had been captured a few days before.

" 2. The Commander-in-Chief wired to say he was pleased to confer the Distinguished Conduct Medal upon No 2170 Cpl. R. EVANS 1st Bn HERTS REGT.

" 3. The Battalion was relieved by the 2nd Bn GRENADIER GUARDS.
On relief the 1st Bn KINGS ROYAL RIFLES were attacked and the two HERTS. Machine Guns which were temporarily attached to the KINGS ROYAL RIFLES got quite a good target.
The Battalion marched back to BETHUNE.

Oct. 8. A draft of 55 men and one Officer (conducting) joined the Battalion from the 11th ENTRENCHING BATTALION.

" 17. The Battalion marched to billets just outside GONNEHEM.

" 21. The Battalion marched into billets at ANNEQUIN.

" 24. The Battalion relieved the 5th Bn KINGS LIVERPOOL REGT. in A.1. Section.

" 26. The following Officers joined the Battalion:-
    2nd LIEUT. C. H. GIMINGHAM.
    "   "   J. W. SMITH.
    "   "   H. SYMONS.

" 27. The Battalion was relieved by the 1st Bn ROYAL BERKS. REGT. and marched back to billets at BEUVRY.
A draft of 20 men arrived from ROUEN.

                         [signature] Lieut-Col.
31/10/15.   Comdg. 1st Bn Herts. Regt.

1915.
Oct 30. 2nd Lieut LEE was wounded in bomb accident, also 6 other ranks.

6th Infantry Brigade.
2nd Division.

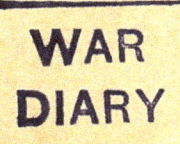

1st BATTN. THE HERTFORDSHIRE REGIMENT.

NOVEMBER

1915

1st Bn. Hertfordshire R-t J.F.

War Diary for November 1915

Nov. 1. Capt E.C.W. PHILLIPS joined the Battalion from No.4 Entrenching Battalion.

" 2. The Battalion relieved the 5th Kings (Liverpool) Regiment in the Trenches astride the LA BASSEE ROAD.

" 3. A draft of 50 men joined Battalion from ROEUN.

" 6. The Battalion was relieved at 1 p.m. by the 5th Scottish Rifles T.R. and marched to billets in ANNEQUIN.

" 7. Marched to billets at GONNEHEM.

" 11. The Battalion was inspected by Lt General GOUGH V.C. on the anniversary of their entering into action at YPRES (11th Nov. 1914).

" 13. The Battalion moved from GONNEHEM to billets at ANNEQUIN.

" 16. The Battalion went into the Trenches in the Brigade Support area, Y4 and Z.C. subsections and relieved the 5th Kings (Liverpool) Regiment NORTH EAST of VERMELLES

1915
Nov. 20. The Battalion was relieved by the KINGS ROYAL RIFLES and relieved the 2nd Bn. SOUTH STAFFORDS in Z.O. Subsector in front line.
21. One Company of the 18th Battalion ROYAL FUSILIERS was attached to the Battalion for instruction in Trench warfare.
22. A second Company of the 18th Battalion ROYAL FUSILIERS was attached for instruction in Trench Warfare.
23. The Battalion was relieved by the 5th Battn KINGS (LIVERPOOL) Regt and marched to billets at ANNEQUIN FOSSE Cottages.
26. The Battalion relieved the 5th KINGS (LIVERPOOL) Regt in Z.O. front line.
" 29. The Battalion was relieved by the 2nd SOUTH STAFFORDS & marched back to billets in the ORPHANAGE, BETHUNE.

J Bevan
Capt & Adjt
1st Bn Herts Regt

1.12.1915.

6th Infantry Brigade.
2nd Division.

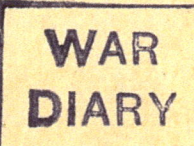

1st BATTN. THE HERTFORDSHIRE REGIMENT.

DECEMBER

1915

Army Form C. 211

WAR DIARY
or
INTELLIGENCE SUMMARY.
(Erase heading not required.)

Instructions regarding War Diaries and Intelligence Summaries are contained in F. S. Regs., Part II. and the Staff Manual respectively. Title pages will be prepared in manuscript.

Hour, Date, Place	Summary of Events and Information	Remarks and references to Appe
2nd December 1915	The Battalion relieved the 2nd SOUTH STAFFORDS in L.O.	
5th	The Battalion was rather heavily shelled this morning on entry having 2 casualties. Battalion was relieved by the 2nd SOUTH STAFFORDS and marched back to billets at MONTMORENCY BARRACKS BETHUNE	
8th	The Battalion relieved the 2nd SOUTH STAFFORDS in Z.	
11th	The Battalion was relieved by the 2nd SOUTH STAFFORDS and marched back to billets at ANNEQUIN	
14th	The Battalion relieved the 1st KINGS in Z.8 (reference at 42I641 (BETHUNE Sheet edition 4.B.200)	
17th	The Battalion was relieved by the 1st ROYAL BERKS and marched back to billets in BETHUNE	
18th	The whole Brigade was relieved by the 95th Brigade. Christmas Day was spent in BETHUNE.	
27th	The Battalion marched back to billets in former ARTOIS	

K.Cash Cpt
M. Herts

6th Brigade

2nd DIVISION.

1st BATTALION

HERTFORDSHIRE REGIMENT

JANUARY 1916.

Army Form C. 2118.

WAR DIARY
or
INTELLIGENCE SUMMARY.
(Erase heading not required.)

Instructions regarding War Diaries and Intelligence Summaries are contained in F.S. Regs., Part II. and the Staff Manual respectively. Title pages will be prepared in manuscript.

Hour, Date, Place	Summary of Events and Information	Remarks and references to Appendices
Dec 9/10/15 to Jany 15th 1916	The Battalion marched back to Lillers in 4am EN RETOIS. Remained there training until the return to Battalion.	
Jany 15. 1916	Moved to Billets at Bethune near the station. The following Officers joined the Battalion – Lieut E.R. Bowes, 2nd Lieut F.C. Eske, A. Eagle, & F.M. Brenadow.	
Jany 18. 1916	The Battalion moved into the Cuinchy area at Givenchy. 2nd Lts G.H. Emmerton & Karr Quentin were relieved by the 6th FSEX (T) Regt marched to relieve 1st Queens at Sector B3. Lieut A McAdine joined the Battalion from St Cowerlag	
Jany 20. 1916	Battalion at Le Quesnoy. F. Coy 2nd ESSEX 1/13 1st Scots Neuves Rd (N St?) Sector B3.	
Jany 23rd 1916	13 Scots (Batt.) 1/9 Det and a Capt B Scots relieved 13 Scots (Lieut Brz) to 104 Scott (MG) 4pm Sub section B3.	
Jany 26. 1916	His Majesty the King inspected the Forces sent to [?] Bullies of Quinchiennes Burt & Sis.	
Jany 27. 1916	The Battalion was relieved by 2nd Scotts Regt – B3 Coy. GIVENCHY and sent in support.	
Jany 30. 1916	The Battalion were relieved by 2nd Cold'm G'ds in Support and marched back to billets in Le Quesnoy	

Hour, Date, Place	Summary of Events and Information	Remarks and references to Appendices
Jany 3? 1916	Draft of 50 NCO's & Men arrived	
Jany 7. 1916	Draft 1/10 " " "	
	The following appeared in the New Years Gazette & Honours	
	Decoration Military Cross.	
	Capt Eaton A.S. Que Oliphant R.M.	
	D.C.M.	
	" R/Major Cpl/Major Grant	
	3630. Pte. Hagger	
	4470 " Fairclough	
	" Mentioned in Despatches. O. Hithcoe [?] Hithcoe [?]	
	3297 Pte! 5th Young G.	
	2190 Oterg " Evans	
	11785 Pte Collins [?]	
	2656 " Fleuria	
	2130 " Suno [?]	

6th Brigade
2nd Division.

BATTALION WENT TO G. H. Q. 21st FEBRUARY 1916.

1st BATTALION

HERTFORDSHIRE REGIMENT

FEBRUARY 1916.

Army Form C. 2118.

WAR DIARY
or
INTELLIGENCE SUMMARY.
(Erase heading not required.)

Instructions regarding War Diaries and Intelligence Summaries are contained in F.S. Regs., Part II. and the Staff Manual respectively. Title pages will be prepared in manuscript.

Hour, Date, Place	Summary of Events and Information	Remarks and references to Appendices
February 2nd 1915 3.0	The Battalion relieved the 10th Hussars in G.2 Givenchy section	
" 5	The Brigade was relieved by the 99 Brigade & 83 Givenchy section	
" 6	The Battalion being relieved by the 1st Bat. followed to the trenches & billets at LINDETTE.	
" 7	Lieut Briggs appointed Machine Gun O.C. & N.Peary O.M.G. vice Reardon	
	assumed command of C Coy of Brigade	
	Sec Lieut L. F. Perry R.E. to Coy S.R. Reardon	
" 8	" Capt E. Q. Gore transferred to B Company	
" 9	" Ordered into billets in support of Brigade in trenches at FESTUBERT	
" 10	The Battalion was relieved at F ESCO Post & moved to be trained	
	at LE TOURET	
" 15	Battalion marched to Billettes at RINETTES	
" 16	Battalion resumed training	
" 17	"	
" 18	" 2nd Lieut R.S. Robinson	
	" Lieutenant was invalided 2nd Lieut R.D. Fearing joined from	
	" and 2nd Lieut Walter V.B. Chamberlayne	
" 19	Battalion marched to La Gorgue and then moving into billets	
	at Rue des CRUELODESQUES near KALMES	
" 20	The Battalion marched to & took over the trenches of 6 B.C.C. 1st Brigade	
" 22	The battalion came in to rest at R.P. 6 B.C.C. 1st Brigade	

Frank [signature]

www.ingramcontent.com/pod-product-compliance
Lightning Source LLC
Chambersburg PA
CBHW081506160426
43193CB00014B/2605